STATE OF SURRENDER

POEMS AND PRAYERS

BY BRETT COSTELLO

❤ Heart Publishers
P.O. Box 4252
Key West, Florida 33041-4252

Book 2, Published 2000
Look for book 3, *Falling Into Grace*

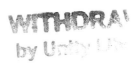
4/0ᴦ

CONTENTS

In this book the words You, Your, Light and Source are capitalized when used in reference to God.

Where are You Now

Where are You now
Your face is not seen.

I saw You yesterday
in the morning dew
and in the winding
trunk of a banyan tree.

I felt Your pulse
in a fist full of ground
and the sway of the mighty sea.

I saw You in a baby's eyes
alive with awe and wonder
content just to be

I felt You in the warm sun
on my skin
and in the soft warm breeze

I saw You shine vivid
in brilliant hibiscus
that to my tired eyes
I no longer see

A part of me has died again
How is it I keep going back
to these things I want
and think I need.

Forgetting again forgetting
I keep giving You away
and losing me.

Turtles

Turtles and I have a lot in common.
The hard, strong shell that keeps us out,
becomes their refuge when trouble is near.

My outer shell that I thought was protection
Keeping You out is my demise
It keeps me from finding
the place where my safety lies.

It's not this outer shell
that makes us the same,
But the love that stirs
deep inside.

Loves Ocean

As each wave rolls in
and then draws back

I can feel the pull
Beckoning me to surrender
and let go into this moment.

Where I lose myself in
Loves ocean.

Fog

Your peace and love move in
like fog off the ocean.

I feel You move in and around me
and suddenly You become
the breath I breathe.

One Cause

Grounded to this earth
the same earth we all walk
connected to each other in love.

Knowing the whole world
just by being here
feeling connected to all

Leaving judgement behind
and realizing the Truth

There is but one cause
to love and assist one another
in this passage called life.
For that truly is life in its
most abundant sense.

Amen

Your World

As each breath
feeds me

I find myself
here again in
Your World

The heavy hand
of desire
has been lifted
in this eternal moment

The ache inside
that always breaks me
has again drawn me
back into Your grace.

Hummingbird

A hummingbird hovers over a deep purple flower.
Drawing up the nectar so sweet.

Her long slender beak designed to
draw out the sweetness.

Her vibration so high
and her wings are buzzing.

Such a beautiful creature,
where did she come from?

God must have put her here for pure delight.

Or maybe she is Nature's tiny angel
with transparent wings and clear vivid sight.

Loves Essence

Thank you for the breath
that wakes me

The sorrow
that breaks me

In my surrender
the essence of
Loves healing power

Flows in and through
and recreates me.

My Place

I claim my place
in this world

On a night
as free as this

Not wanting to
be known by anyone

Now knowing myself
by this flowing
within me.

Drawn Deeper

The sea is moved
back and forth
between continents
in a flowing motion
it caresses each shore

Its wet cool touch
soothes the hot sand
and those with fiery souls

The mystery she holds
leaves us in awe and wonder.

We feel her depth
and are drawn deeper
to our own.

Nothing to Do

Free of anything to do
or where to go

Birds swoop overhead
in graceful flight
playing and singing
in a great blue sky

On the dock
tide has risen full
the smell of seawater
fills the air.

Lying on warm grass
near the garden

Flowers by the thousands
magnificent colors
different shapes and forms

Bees filling themselves
with their sacred sweetness

This day a blessed offering
for those of us
free of anything to do
in this moment.

Where we have no place to go.

A Dream or Being

As I stood looking
the beauty of the
painting drew me in

Into the river
with the wildflowers stretched
along the banks

Bright and vivid
millions of colored hands
reaching out to me

The wind calls me closer
I feel myself falling in

Am I in the middle
of a dream.

Or in the middle of being
awakening to what I am.

Ripe Fruit

Fruit bears itself
and wets my lips
with its ripe sweetness

Gifts for no reason
fall into my hands

Every feeling or thought
of pain
has been taken from me
and replaced with
this perfect song

When it sings inside
all my cares melt
in this welcoming place
I know I am Home.

Amen

Faith

We sat quietly
never saying a word
our heavy hearts
did all the talking

Tears of uncertainty
and of longing
in our parting
both of our hearts
feeling frail and torn

I know I must leave here
and follow in faith
even though my heart
is afraid and not sure.

Undo these Knots

Make my life shine

Let it reflect
a pure clear image
of what I am

Open my heart
let it Love,
undo these knots
I carry inside

Let me feel
Your sweet presence
that makes me feel alive.

Amen

Wind

The wind, like a pump, blasting itself
onto everything in its reach.

The house is shaking.
My house is shaking
from the whirlwind in my soul.

Churning up my emotions
and spitting them out leaving me empty
as the trees outside

The old fruitage is being stripped away
to make room for the fresh, fruit to grow.

Lying dormant, waiting to be filled back up
with new life and vision.

The wait can be cold, fearful and lonely.
It can seem like it may not come

Just as the tree knows
we also have been made a promise
and it will come,
yes it will come.

Creation

How the heart opens
in the beauty of creation

You push the spring buds
open with Your breath.

Birds sing in ecstacy
from the gentle touch
that springtime brings.

New green things all around
rising up from the
moist rich ground.

Flowering every bud flowering
no struggle
They're already surrendered.

No place to get to
They're already home.

When Gods love opens my heart
my emotions take me
in this moment when

I remember.

Spirits Awakened

Two turtles sitting on a log
in the warm summer sun
side by side with their heads pulled in
close to the waters edge
withdrawn from their surroundings.

Suddenly the turtle closest to
the water feels a stirring inside
The warmth from the sun penetrates
his shell he has an urge to look around.

Out comes his head and it's as if
his eyes are open for the first time.

Everything in sight is vibrant and clear
he feels Love pouring out of him
alive with energy and light.

Suddenly the other turtle feels
his energy and is drawn out.

In an instant both full of joy
are dancing together on the log.

Full of Love and Life.
Free as a breeze.

With You I Bend

My rising spirit
never looks back
to where its been.

In this place
I'm lifted above
the part of me
that sometimes feels afraid.

You show me myself
in a way
where there is
no room to look
upon this world
with discouragement and hate.

Here where I bend
like a reed in the wind
fresh and green
accepting what comes.

When I am here
I could hardly break.

Caught

I'm caught, snatched up in it,
Chained to my fears, forgetting,
Like a vulture frantically tearing
at a dead carcass.

I scurry and grab,
frantic and afraid.

I'm snatched up, my heart opens
and the possibilities are infinite.

How could I be looking through the same eyes.
These eyes are clear and don't struggle
with difference but find only beauty.

This is how I long to see,
Through the eyes of God.

Gods Gift

God has given
every creature
a different way
of providing.

The pelican with its
long bill and quickness
snatches fish from the sea.

While the sandpiper
with its long legs
wades in the shallows
stalking its prey.

Fish feed on one another
where the hunter
in an instant
can become the prey

This natural state
where everything flows
is where I arrive
when I connect
with Your magic

I know I am home.

Morning

The kiss of sunlight
shines through green trees.

Morning awakens the coo
from inside the dove.

I take the time to be still
and embrace the coo
of my own heart
before my fears
can hush her song.

Delicate flowers sway in the breeze
warmed by dawns touch.

The pull of the day
takes me out into
the world.

Where I find You everywhere
In these moments of remembering.

Your Life

Clear and blue
water or sky

Up or down
left or right

I see fish fly
and birds dive

take a breath
this is your
Life.

The Reef

Slapping the hull of
my small boat
on choppy waters

Trying to make my way
through waves and wind
to the rich reef
where fish are abundant.

My mind gets stuck
on reaching my destination
suddenly I've lost myself.

Then I notice the pink sky
and dark clouds moving
with the wind

A beautiful turquoise sea
The taste on my lips
from the salty spray

I'm drawn back into
the heaven of the moment
where in this opening

I feel my connection
to all of this.

Waking Moments

Dawn has arrived again
that sweet freshness
comes pouring through
in these waking moments
with You.

Alive

A bird gracefully lands
on the tree branch
still and alert
she sings her song
with no worry
of what's to come.

Alive in this moment
where she and the branch
are the love.

In an Instant

When I awoke
on this morning
feeling my heart heavy.

Were there not a kernel
of new hope hidden away.

A spark of knowing
that in one instant
it could all change.

I wouldn't be able to get up
and greet this day.

There's a wisdom that speaks
even in my pain.

Though my faith is weak
and my heart feels frayed.

As I walk this path
the door to my soul will open
revealing Your face.

These unbearable moments
that I'm stuck in
will seem so far away.

All my Heart

You are my rock
my strength and courage.

You are my joy,
my hope and vision.

You are the love
that stirs inside me.

Your love, the perfection
I strive to stay in.

This is the life
I've been chosen to live.

With all of my heart
and with each breath I take

I will live it.

Amen

Against all Odds

The wind carries a seed
it lands on rough broken concrete
of an abandoned bridge miles from shore.

Longing to find a place
where it can be nourished and grow.

One more gust of wind
the seed is pushed into a small crack
where bits of dirt and water collect.

The seed takes root
against all odds begins to grow.

Over the years a
beautiful green bush has emerged.

Miles from land
but never alone.

In springtime a delicate
pink flower blooms
from her lush green branches.
Her beauty is fully exposed.

We are always provided
with the love that's needed.

For those of us who long
with an ache in our hearts
and the willingness
to take root and grow.

The same love that
carried that seed
and gave it life.

Will lift you higher
and carry you home.

Waters Edge

April evening
in this island town
the wind rustles
in the palms.

Children explore
the sandy beach
making new discoveries
like little pilgrims
full of excitement and awe

Birds gracefully glide overhead
some make their way
along the shore
each with its own way of being
having its own song.

The salty smell in the air
draws my attention
to the waters edge.

The waters edge
where the suns reflection
reveals Your grace.

Where now I feel drawn
into Your ocean.

When Hearts Touch

She wore the days joy
with the grace
of a gentle cool rain
opening flowers in spring.

Her words sweet and calm
like a clear mountain spring
bubbling from the ground.

In her moment of innocence
Lets go of the need

To be any particular way.

Hearts sometimes touch
when its least expected
in the most mysterious ways.

Who are You

The world is my womb
on this fearless night
I know from this warmth inside
that You are near.

Peace was defined
by this feeling
even the flowers
across the walkway
see it in me.

The palm tree waves freely
in the open air.

My pen slides across this paper
by a guided hand.

In each new face
that passes by
You shine back to me.

Who are You?
The One that
shows me to myself.

My Body

My body talks to me
of the changes going on.

When I climb back into my head
my body tells me it's so.

When I can just live
for that place in my heart
I'm freed from these judgements
they all lose their hold.

I become open and free.
Where this love is my home.

RYAN COSTELLO

Honey Bee

The honey bee was buzzing
with delight
drawing the sweet nectar
from this delicate flower.

The flower relaxes
and gladly gives to the bee
what it needs
never worrying
that he'll take too much.

We should live
with such giving and trust.

Reaching You

I want to write words
that reach inside.

Touching that place in you
that's been forgotten.

A place where
everything we are
has been hiding

And all we need
Lives there.

A fathomless ocean
where there is no drowning.

A filling presence
where shackles of the past

And barred windows
of the future

Are all erased
from our thought

Where in this moment
we rest in this boundless Love
That has long been aching
to be found.

The Garden

A delicate web
of color and light.

The busy bee visits
newly opened blossoms
with sheer delight.

Knowing this sweetness
is what keeps him
in flight.

Haven

Like a small bird
hatched out in a
soft warm nest
tasting the sweetness
of spring.

This world is
woven around me
my heart opens
and I lose myself.

This is my haven
there is none
as sweet and peaceful
as this.

Fasting

My spirit strengthens
as my belly gets emptier.

When those hunger pangs come
and I refuse to give into them
my fear and stored up grief
come out in a river of tears
and empty me.

In the emptiness
suddenly there's an opening
and everything comes alive.

Birds singing in unison
the wind in the palms.

Clouds moving across the sky
as I feel myself moved by them.

The oceans wet kiss on the shore.

Light flickering across the water
as the sun cuts a pathway of light.

Then sinks down and makes room
for the night.

Passage

My inward journey
takes me through
many dark valleys
and over many
high mountain peaks.

This narrow path
sometimes winding
then it's straight again.

Each step
I take in faith
weaves an elegant pattern.

In the fabric
of my Life.

Amen

Between the Fear

Emptying, I keep emptying,
my face wet with tears.

A voice inside cries out,
be with the love
in the spaces between your fear.

Free falling into them,
I keep falling into them.

Trusting, yes trusting,
until this loving space
is where I live.

Frozen

In the cold winter, the river freezes,
creating the illusion that it stopped.
But underneath, it secretly makes its way
in a continuous flow.

So, it is with me when I'm frozen in my fear.
I lose my trust and pain moves in,
forgetting You are near.

Your movement from within is
what I long to feel.
So, I wait in quiet
Knowing Your love will flow
when the truth
is once again revealed.

I Forget

I set out
to find God,
miracles unfold ,
signs on the road
then I forget
my purpose
in my confusion
my wanting grows
cutting me off
stopping Gods flow.

Knowing Myself

God speaks to me
gentle and loving
from this empty place.

Knowing the depth
and dark places
my heart has been.

Giving me strength
to go into the night.

So I may remember
and know myself again.

The Cure

In a world of frustration
where we keep reaching out there
and come back with empty hands.

So quick to take the cure
slow to look inside.

So much to do
just to stay alive.

So little faith
with no place left to hide.

A new name for the fear
that gets pushed down
and held inside.

A new pill
to take away the pain
it's like the resurrection
another God has arrived.

We've become so afraid
of the darkness.

We give our strength away
believing in these lies
not knowing what we are inside
If we keep pushing
down the darkness

The sun within
will never rise.

When I See

The wind that moves
while plants dance
to Your touch.

Birds glide
in effortless flight.

The river that runs through
unleashed in her passage.

Winding and flowing
toward her ocean home.

The ground that nourishes
and feeds

The sun that draws
them out of themselves.

This the Love
I feel so deeply
when I truly see
I am in God's Flow.

Amen

So Much to Gain

A thousand trees sway and talk
leaves fall from their branches

as they become bare and empty
no more distractions

bark and branch
wind and rain
roots deeply planted
in rich dark vein

inside life thrives
as sap runs through

within themselves in this quiet time
of reflection

Nothing expected and so much
to gain.

A Night Like This

Lonely, not on a night
like this
the clouded stream
is running clear again.

A whole universe
within me
on such a night.

Stars sparkle and shine
as if they knew me.
Full moon winks.

Cool night air
still and quiet
breathes slowly
through the darkness.

The new dawn breaks.
Hope blossoms.
Joy fills my heart
as I feel You come closer.

Ship of Fear

One more stone
thrown on board
my sinking ship
of disappointment
as we sail toward
deep water.

She takes on more water
sluggish in her movement
cursing this ship
go down you floundering
vessel go down.

This sinking is worse
than the drowning itself.

Sink oh ship of fear
to the deepest depths
so that my mighty spirit
may rise again.

Nagging Ache

Depression and how it creeps in.

Nagging ache, grey empty stare
through hazy windows.

Like a fog pushing in
along the shore.

Heavy breath
no sense of direction
and no sign of dawn.

In the distance
a light in a tower
sounding a bell.

I just need to listen
and it will lead me home.

Awakened Moment

I have never found God
in any particular place.

It is only in my state of surrender
that I am drawn into
the awakened moment,

where God lives in me.

River

Love runs wild
to an open heart

Like the river
runs to its
ocean home.

Bright Star

A life, A breath
A gasp, then death

A mountain peak
the warm sun
Your open heart
need not run

A valley, the night
makes me quiver from inside

Your touch that wakes me
Your leaving that leaves me aching

My soul the ground
all the life that takes root there

Your grace the Ocean
my love there that opens

This world my hope
of where Im being led to
the bright star
that sparkles and shines
shows me
how to be.

True Place

A deep wish lies in my heart
in my secret prayer

A life that goes beyond the stars
in my secret prayer

A life full of love and caring
in my secret prayer

A clear reflection of who I am
in my secret prayer

A peaceful home with loving friends
in my secret prayer

A devotion to God that never ends
In my secret prayer

Sharing my love with all the world
sharing my innermost self
by revealing these words
being here now
just awaiting Gods word

In my secret prayer

Amen

Loves Embrace

Springs warm breath
on my face.

Lost in this beauty
that surrounds me
every turn I take

The vast ocean
as far a I can see

The soothing sound of each wave
with new life all around
each revealing its face.

Seen for what they are
so connected
free and easy
calm and safe

No struggles or
feelings of disgrace

Just a flowing that comes
by giving into grace

Reminding me to open
and accept Loves embrace.

Closer to Yourself

Turn around
look where you've been.

Your persistence has
kept you moving

Another step closer
to yourself.

Just when you were
ready to throw up
your hands.

God whispered a secret
and another part
of you awakens.

Opening your world.

A new feeling of hope
and gratitude for this
breath of life that comes
in this remembering place.

Heaven in Your Heart

Your sparkle, the twilight
the stars above you

Your laughter, God's joy
the heaven in your heart

Your smile the sun
warmth and light
from where did you come

Your Faith and trust
of where you're going

Carry you gracefully
On wings, through the world.

Wind Storm

Wind hard and strong
puffing and blasting

Like a serpent
demanding we take notice

The powerful breath
moves and shakes
uprooting and rousting
the soul of man and beast
scouring this crust of earth.

Water spouts shoot up
from a turbulent sea

While birds fold their wings
and hold on tight

And angels soar
into the night

She won't give in,
relentlessly pushing and shouting

You will awaken
I will awaken you

Get up from your
deep sleep.

Walls

A lifetime spent building them,
this wall I hide behind.

In the moment that
the truth is revealed,
I slam the door shut
for fear that my
whole world will crumble
leaving me helpless
and alone.

Building a stronger defense
never knowing myself
just this hunger for power,
money, and control
to protect the lie I've bought
taking me further away
from my soul.

Layer upon layer
on the crumbling wall
never feeling my connection
to loves power.

The walls are too tall.

In my secret prayer,
I yearn for it to fall
opening my heart
letting love flow.

Your Shore

Your miracles
I'll never understand

I never seem to know
when You're coming or going

When I feel You
I welcome this miracle
and honor Your presence.

When I think You've gone
I flounder and thrash
in deep water.

Drowning in these
waves of fear
drifting further away

From Your Shore

Amen

From Myself

This brokenness is
the moment I live in

This is where my
yearning cries out from

I carry this inside
and in the stillness
it can't be ignored.

This busy world
has lost its power
to push it away.

Those old distractions
can't keep me from myself
anymore.

Flame

Sometimes like a wild fire,
inside Your flame burns
You roar in my soul

Other times just a flicker
never penetrating
my icy walls
so thick so cold

I reach not knowing
how I've fallen
from the fire
of Your Love.

Amen

After the Storm

Half mast
she floundered
in a calming sea
after the storm
torn sails and
a badly beaten hull

Heading toward port
to rest and repair
the damaged body
that weathered the storm

That through grace

Has been shown
the way back
Home.

Ryan

Light hearted and witty
his joy and humor
is an art.

Sometimes in his grasping
for what he thinks he needs,
his innocence gets lost

Reminding me of myself
when I get caught.

He is a priceless gift
teaching me as I teach him
that loving without conditions
is not always easy
and can only be done
when I slow down enough
to see him

Laying aside my ego
that keeps me stuck
in right and wrong

Creating a space
where the heart
can speak
to the heart.

In and Out of Myself

I wander in and out of being
It doesn't matter what people think
then it does.

I feel trusting and guided
then I don't.

I see all the doors opening
then I feel trapped between two
that have slammed shut.

I'm free then bound within
the chains of my mind.

I expand out into the universe
then contract and become small.

I feel loves power
and then fears prison.

I remember my name
and then forget.

But You always remind me
You keep reminding me.

One day I will not
remember to forget.

Amen

No Prayer

Full moon night
naked sky
glorifies her light

Breeze touching my skin
making it real

Gods love touching my heart
making it feel

So many souls
making their way

There are the light ones,
some heavy and grey

There is hope in the air
on this glorious night

Even for those with
no prayer to pray.

Her Grace

She stood on the shore
her long silky dress
pushed up against her
milky white legs.

As the breeze pushes
its way in,
salty and cool,
touching her skin.

Slipping out of her shoes
raising her dress up around
soft white thighs.

Such beauty gracefully wading in
with a solemn but light way about her,
as if while standing in her own reflection.

Seeing clearly the changes
and remembering where she has been.

Life's Balance

Gods breath, my heart
the deep blue sky

The ocean moving and flowing
the life beneath its surface
and the breath of life up above.

The clouds, and the sun
streaming through them.

The ground, and the way
it draws me into myself.

Lifes balance, and my soul
that only wants to know You.

This world the place I walk
in shadow and light.

The joy of this moment
and the hope and faith I have
of the life that's yet to come.

My Hearts Night

If I had never
walked through my
hearts night.

How could I know
Your sun?

If I were never lost,
How could I have
found myself in You?

If I were never dying
with a thirst
for God's touch,

How could I have surrendered
and let Your Love
wash over me?

Being at the bottom
creates my passage
to the top.

Night leads me
to dawn

An ache in my heart
becomes the cure.

By continually dying
my soul is born.

Amen

Into Myself

As the sunset passes
before me
on this
still cool night
I settle down
into myself
where my heart
feels safe
in this place
of peace where
I'm unafraid of
the night.

Bird Song

You sing so sweetly
outside my window,
even on a day
as gray as this.

The others are not singing
the way I hear them
on those bright sunny mornings.

Maybe this gray day
has got them down.

It's not that way
with you though.

Whether it's gray or bright
something inside
seems to keep you singing.

Song of Creation

In the center
of the opening bud
where the sweetest
part of the flower
in spring comes alive.

There's a song
that it sings
when the sun's
warm touch
is felt deep inside.

It's the song
of creation
the one we all sing.

When we are blessed
by the grace
of remembering.

And our spirit feels alive.

Familiar Place

She sat close to me
looking on and listening
both of us
in that timeless state

The place where
truth is deeply felt
and we open
trusting and safe

Through her eyes
I see the love
in her soul.

Taking me back
I connect with my own.
Embracing this moment
when loves power
has taken me
to this familiar
but uncommon place.

Angel

An angel lands
on my shoulder
and whispers God's message
healing my heart
taking my pain
setting me free
I feel whole again

Amen

Lifting and Holding

I love how I'm touched.

Like the breeze
neath the wings of a dove.

Lifting and holding
her steady.

I'm left with this feeling
that comes from within.

Peaceful and Safe
Opened to Your Love.

Is That You

I thought I knew
the sound of Your voice.

When to move
and when to stay.

I was happy there
feeling guided and safe.

Somehow Your message
to me got crossed.

Or maybe it was
something I wanted
that pushed it away.

I just know one thing,
the sound of Your voice
would be sweet and welcomed.

When we are apart
I'm lost in these feelings.

Please say something
I can't bear this pain.

Love Inside

There's a dove inside
that wants to be free.

She opens her wings
then you crush her,
with some mean talk
some wanting or hatred
something in the past
you can't let go.

But still inside
she sings her song
you can't kill her
or dampen her spirit,
this is the voice of your soul.
And you can only ignore
her presence for so long.

She'll spread her wings again
and await the day
Love opens the way
for her to fly off.

Half Blind

I find myself
in this world

not always seeing
half blind

walking
I keep walking

yearning
I'm still yearning

searching
I keep searching

little by little
opening out

I see
and then I don't

I'm alive
and then die again

I'm here now
where You live in me

Then falling away
into time and space.

It Happened Over Time

I hadn't known
it happened over time
so slowly I had died

I couldn't feel
the depth of my pain
nor the joy and wonder
within my soul.

The birds had stopped singing,
the mountain streams laughter was gone.

The air still and heavy,
no connection to trees or ground.

Blossoming flowers, the buzzing bees
full of sweet nectar,
held no place in my heart.

My awe of the birds in flight,
in flight is where I need to go.

A universe full of mystery,
somehow I had lost the way.

I had not the time to take in
the fragrance and beauty
of the garden or the rose.

You awakened me
to a place inside
I had forgotten,
it seemed so long ago.

I've come alive in my joy
and my pain.

I would never give away
Your precious gift.

Ever in my darkest night
for that dull sense of existence
that for so many years
stood by my door.

Tide Within

The shadow
veiling my heart
is easing its way out
back into the night
where it has a place to belong.

That damp cold chill
and the ache inside leave me
as the turning tide within changes.

The spark inside grows
to a flame
with my remembrance
of You.

With each breath
I am drawn
into this moment.

Where something new
lives in me.

Amen

Absence of Your Love

Heavy heart bearing down hard
on my innermost being.

A well of tears
covering my unknown fears.

Walking in icy streams
feeling naked and cold.

Not knowing myself
split off all alone.

Forgetting I keep forgetting
so empty and lost.

Scratching my way
consumed in this pain.

Reaching for a thread of truth
that might pull me back,

And stitch up this wound,
this empty, gaping hole,

that is always present.

In the absence of Your Love.

Like They Are

Small birds
stand on a stone
near the shore

In a setting sun
the tide makes its way in.

Waves splash
onto the shore
each playing a part
in the rhythm.

Why can't I be
more like they are
always so connected
peaceful and trusting
accepting what comes
with each moment.

A life with such
Freedom and Grace

Falling From My Perch

When the faithful have lost faith
and the hopeful have no hope

The dreamer has stopped dreaming
and has lost his vision

The cord is cut,
fearful and alone.

When the deep seeded hurt
is the only voice I hear

I've fallen from my perch
filled with the grief of things lost
and things that haven't come.

These lowly times when I question
even You my God.

Through all this darkness
and shattered brokenness
when I've had enough and
can't take anymore.

Quietly through a crack
Your love comes streaming through
and speaks to my heart.
All this thrashing and tearing
is healed once more.

In this moment
by the presence of

Your Powerful Love.